WHO WAS...

KING HENRY VIII

The Exploding King

EMMA CRAIGIE

Illustrations by Alex Fox

＊ SHORT BOOKS

First published in 2006 by Short Books
15 Highbury Terrace
London N5 1UP

10 9 8 7 6 5 4 3 2 1

A CIP catalogue record for this book
is available from the British Library.

Illustration copyright © Alex Fox 2006
Quiz by Sebastian Blake

ISBN 1-904977-57-X

Printed and bound in Great Britain by
Bookmarque Ltd., Croydon, Surrey

For my mother, Gillian Rees-Mogg, who looked after my children so that I could write this book.

CHAPTER ONE
Death

The night of the 27th of January 1547 was colder than any we have ever known. All the rivers of Europe were frozen. In the vast Whitehall Palace, beside the icy Thames, Henry VIII lay feverish in his great gold painted-bed.

He was not an easy patient. His huge body was impossibly heavy. For months he had been unable to haul himself about and special machines had been devised to lift him on to his horse, to winch him up the stairs and even to carry him from room to room. Now he was in bed it was back-breaking work to shift him to a comfortable position. Then there was the smell. On each thigh, large open ulcers seeped and pussed and stank. But worst was his temper. Henry's doctors knew he was dying, and that he needed to prepare his soul for death or risk eternal hell. But they were too scared to tell him. Henry had always hated any mention of death and had declared that anyone found guilty of predicting the death of the King would be hanged, drawn and quartered. In other words: the offender would be hanged briefly, then cut down whilst still alive; his innards would be cut out and his genitals cut off and burnt in front of him. Only then would he be killed: his head cut off and his body chopped into quarters.

Very bravely, Sir Anthony Denny, Henry's chief servant, approached the groaning King. Bowing deeply, Denny gave his warning: "In man's judgement, your majesty is not likely to live. The time has come to remember your sins like every good Christian man."

Henry sighed: "Like all men I admit that I have sinned, yet is the mercy of Christ able to pardon me all my sins, though they were greater than they be."

"Would your majesty like to speak with any learned man?"

"Would it were Thomas Cranmer, but I will first take a little sleep, and then, as I feel myself, I will advise upon the matter." He closed his eyes.

A couple of hours later, barely waking, the King

stirred and called for Cranmer, the Archbishop of Canterbury. Cranmer was in Croydon, so he came on horseback. It was a slow journey on the icy roads and by the time he finally arrived, Henry was barely conscious.

Cranmer took the King's hand and spoke gently to the dying man: "Your majesty, show me some sign that you have put your trust in the mercy of God, through Jesus Christ. Henry squeezed Cranmer's hand "as hard as he could". It was his final gesture. At two in the morning on the 28th of January 1547, King Henry VIII died. He was 55 years old.

By the time he died, Henry VIII was feared by everyone. He had had six wives, and had executed two of them. He had also executed his closest advisors; his church leaders; most of his cousins; scores of friends and courtiers, and thousands of ordinary people just because they were Scottish, or Catholic, or Protestant, or jobless, or homeless. By some estimates 72,000 people were executed during his reign. That's 2.5% of the population. He was a mass murderer.

When he died no one knew what to do. His courtiers were at a loss without their leader. So they did nothing. They pretended that nothing had happened. For three days Henry's death was kept secret even from his servants. His meals were delivered as usual "to the sound of trumpets". Ambassadors were told he was indisposed. Only on the 31st of January was his death finally announced to parliament, and his nine-year-old son, Edward VI, proclaimed King. Throughout his life Henry had been determined to leave his kingdom in the safe hands of an adult son. He had failed.

CHAPTER TWO
Deterioration

A drawing of Henry at the end of his life shows a hideous man. He appears to be bald beneath his jewel-encrusted hat, and has bizarre pencil-thin eyebrows arching coldly above small, sunken eyes. He has a tight little mouth decked with a dab of moustache, and he seems to have no neck. His vast cheeks are edged by a short, curly beard, which merges with the frills of his lacy collar. Yet in his youth Henry was considered to be a magnificent specimen of a man. According to an Italian agent, he was simply: "the handsomest prince ever seen"!

When Henry VIII became King in 1509 at the age of 17, the country was thrilled. Henry's father, Henry VII, had been a dour man. But Henry VIII was fun-loving and high spirited and full of vim and vigour. As one courtier wrote, "The whole world is rejoicing in the possession of so great a prince... the heavens laugh, the earth exults."

Henry's first act as King was hugely popular: he imprisoned Dudley and Empson, his father's tax collectors, who had been hated by the people for ruthlessly fining and imprisoning people who were too poor to pay the taxes. Later he had them executed. At the same time Henry issued a general pardon and all other prisoners were released. In the words of an ambassador from Venice: "Love for the King is universal with all who see him, as His Highness does not seem a person of this world but one descended from heaven."

Henry had charisma. He had a way of making everyone feel special. People were also very impressed by the fact that he was tall. "Among a thousand noble companions, the King stands out the tallest, and his strength fits his majestic body." He was six foot two, which was unusual for his times. The Spanish ambassador, writing to Katharine of Aragon's father, couldn't help noticing with delight that "his limbs are of gigantic size". How did this handsome prince turn into a demon king?

CHAPTER THREE
Education

Henry VIII had been born in the summer of 1491 in the Palace of Greenwich, beside the river Thames, just down river from London. It was a fairy-tale castle with turrets and spires, courtyards and fountains and misty acres of parkland. He was a bonny, chubby baby, the third child of Henry VII and Queen Elizabeth of York, and their second son. His older brother Arthur was the heir to the throne, and spent his childhood with their father, the King, being groomed for kingship, whilst Henry and his sisters were brought up by their mother and their nanny, Anne Luke.

Henry's mother was a tall, pale, beautiful woman. She was kind and gentle. She loved to tell the children stories: stories of King Arthur and the knights in shining armour, who won glorious jousts and battles; stories of the great Kings of England who fought and beat the French. But Queen Elizabeth of York was often sad. As Henry was growing up his mother was endlessly pregnant, and frequently weeping. One after the other her last four babies died. Henry and his siblings spent most of their time in the ancient house of Eltham Palace, surrounded by a moat. Inside the palace the high stone walls were lined with carpets and tapestries. Blazing fires kept them warm, but there were dark and draughty corridors, hiding places, long shadows cast by the candles that lit them to bed. Huge kitchens provided enormous meals. There were hundreds of servants; a court orchestra, a choir, jesters to entertain them. But beyond the moat, beyond the oak woods and the deer park, lay an uncertain world.

In June 1497 Henry, who was about to be six, was staying at his grandmother's London house with his mother and sisters. Ten-year-old Arthur was, as usual, away with their father, who was preparing for a battle against Scotland. Suddenly the children heard a great commotion – shouting from the hallway, footsteps running up and down the wooden stairs. The servants started rushing about packing up chests of clothes. Outside, the horses whinnied as they were brought from their stables. Their grandmother, Lady Margaret Beaufort, was issuing instructions, calling for litters to be brought: covered chairs for the children to be carried in. Suddenly, Anne Luke ran into the bed chamber "Awake! Make haste!" she called. "We must flee. We must go to the Tower!" As they were bundled into litters, baby Mary began to cry, but she was quickly soothed by the rhythm of the horses, and fell asleep. By the time she awoke they were safely locked into the ancient fortress of the Tower of London. It was a strange place to be. It was the place where the most dangerous prisoners in the land were sent, and many had been executed or murdered there. It was also home to some exotic wild animals: lions, leopards, bears, wolves and lynxes. But it was a royal castle above all, and the safest place for the prince and princesses, when London was under attack.

An army of 15,000 Cornishmen were marching towards the capital city. They had gathered supporters on the way. They were protesting against the huge taxes that the King had demanded from them. The Cornish army had now reached Blackheath, just across the River Thames from the Tower. Henry's father, King Henry VII, was ready for them. He had turned around his own army which had been heading for Scotland.

Reports of what followed vary. There was a battle. Some said 2000 Cornishmen were killed, some said 200. What is certain is that Henry VII's army won. The Cornish leaders were captured, and brought to the Tower's dungeons. The day before Henry's sixth birthday they were tied to wooden pallets and dragged to the place of their execution.

This was not the only time that Henry's father had to crush a rebellion. These were dangerous times. For more than thirty years the country's leading families had been fighting for the throne. Henry's father had won it in battle, becoming the fourth king of England in two years. He never felt safe. There were frequent plots against him. Many people in England thought he had no right to be king. Although he was called Henry VII, he was not descended from the six King Henries who had come before him. But having taken the kingdom by force, he held his power tightly. He was determined to see off all challenges and hand the crown on to his son when he died.

Henry's father was a thin, tense, wiry man who trusted no one. He avoided relying on other people. Late into the night he would sit alone in his chilly chamber, straining his eyes as he pored over the nation's accounts by candlelight. All his hopes for the future were pinned on his son Arthur. The first step was to find Arthur a princess to marry. So at the age of three Arthur was engaged to the Spanish princess, Katharine of Aragon. They married when he was 15 and she was 17. But five months later Arthur, who had always been a weak and skinny boy, was dead. Ten-year-old Henry, now a strapping lad, became heir to the throne. Within a year his broken-hearted mother had also died and Henry was left with his stern and gloomy father.

Henry never went to school or university; he was educated by tutors. Sir Thomas More, who was later Henry's Lord Chancellor, and, later still, executed by him, claimed that Henry had "more learning than any English monarch possessed before him". He was certainly a bright student who, by the age of 18, was fluent in "French, English and Latin, and understands Italian well". He is said to have found mathematics easy. He loved astronomy and all the sciences. He collected scientific instruments, and maps. He designed weapons, ships, fortifications, and palaces. He is said to have read widely, and written beautifully. He loved music. His father gave him a lute when he was seven, and he later gathered a huge collection of musical instruments: 26 lutes as well as trumpets, viols, rebecs, sackbuts, harpsichords and organs, fifes and drums.

Like his father, Henry surrounded himself with musicians throughout his life, maintaining a court orchestra, a choir of 79 singers for the Royal Chapel, as well as six choristers who always travelled with him. He composed music, could sight read and sang with a high voice. He excelled at all the traditional royal sports: tilting, jousting, hunting, archery and tennis. Much less grandly he is known to have played football – a commoner's game – and had boots specially made for him.

Despite all this brilliance, Henry's father did not trust him. He didn't give him any of the training or responsibility that he had given Arthur, and he didn't allow him any freedom. When he was 16, Henry was confined to his tapestried room. From the window he could see the endless stretches of deer park, but he was not allowed into the gardens or parkland unless his father gave permission. Even then he had to be supervised, and to use a private back door, so that he did not mix with visitors to the court. There was no escape. The only way in or out of his room was through his father's bedchamber.

There were mutterings at court. Fuensalida, a visitor from the royal court of Spain, scoffed: "The prince is treated like a young girl. It is never possible to speak with him. He uttereth not one word, unless to answer a question from his father!" One of Henry's cousins, Reginald Pole, thought he knew why Henry's father was so strict: "The King hath no affection or fancy unto him. They quarrelleth so violently that men feareth that the King doth seek to kill his son. The King feareth that his son might obtain too much power, even during his own lifetime."

As it turned out Henry was not to be kept from power for long. Shortly before his 18th birthday his father died. The restrictions were over. Henry VIII was King.

CHAPTER FOUR
Coronation

As soon as his father died, Henry decided to marry his brother's widow, the Spanish princess, Katharine of Aragon. It was a decision which amazed everyone. They had been engaged since he was 12 and she was 17, and she had remained in London for six years waiting to marry him. But there had been a series of hitches, and on the night before his 14th birthday Henry had officially declared that now that he was reaching "the years of puberty" he had decided not to go ahead with the marriage: "I protest vehemently against it and am utterly opposed to it."

There were two further big problems with the marriage. One was money. Henry's father, while he was still alive, had wanted her parents to pay a dowry of

100,000 gold crowns. King Ferdinand agreed to this, but, to Katharine's great embarrassment, he kept failing to pay it.

The other problem was that the marriage was technically illegal. It was against the law of the church for a man to marry his brother's widow. Special permission had to be given by the Pope who was head of the church. By the time the Pope had granted permission, the two fathers, Henry VII and King Ferdinand, had fallen out completely, and Henry VII had started looking for a different wife for his son.

So why did Henry change his mind as soon as his father died? He gave two reasons: he said it had been his father's dying wish, and he told Katharine's father that, in any case, "I would choose her for a wife before all others." At last, King Ferdinand paid the dowry. Henry insisted on cash. Not that he needed it. His careful father had left him a fortune: £1,250,000 – worth about £375 million today.

The marriage took place quietly in the chapel at Greenwich Palace. Ten days later the royal couple rode to the Tower of London and on the 23rd of June 1509 they processed to Westminster for the coronation the following day: old midsummer's day.

London had never seen anything like it. The streets

were lined with tapestries and cloth of gold. Free wine flowed from the public water pipes. The roads were strewn with herbs and flowers. The horses and all the lords and ladies of the court were dressed in scarlet and white and green. Henry, surrounded by bodyguards, rode a richly decorated horse and despite a short, sharp shower, which some took as a bad omen, must have been boiling beneath a robe of crimson velvet, lined with ermine fur and a coat studded with diamonds and emeralds and rubies. Catherine followed, carried in a litter decorated with white silk and gold ribbons. She was dressed all in white; her long hair loose like a bride's, a circlet of gold and pearls upon her head.

In Westminster Abbey, Henry took his coronation oath. He was anointed with holy oil and crowned with a golden crown. The Queen was crowned with a gold diadem spangled with sapphires and rubies and pearls. As the new King and Queen emerged from the Abbey, the crowd cheered wildly; the choir sang alleluiah; the trumpets blasted; the drums rolled; the bells rang out across the city.

The coronation banquet was said to be the greatest feast the world had ever known. The food, "sumptuous, fine and delicate meats", was brought into Westminster Hall on horseback. After the banquet there was a tournament of jousting, then more feasting, more jousting. The party lasted for five days.

Henry was thrilled to be King. He immediately set off on an endless round of sporting and feasting, travelling from palace to palace. On one trip, for instance, it is recorded that he spent his time "in shooting, singing, dancing, wrestling, casting of the bar, playing at the recorders, flute and virginals, and in setting of songs, making of ballads." He was also hunting, hawking, jousting in tournaments, dressing up and performing little plays, playing tennis and cards and dice and spending money: £566 (equivalent to £166,800) on a thousand pearls; over £800, (£240,000) on New Year gifts; and huge amounts were lost gambling: £2 (£600) to a man who won a bet that he could eat a whole deer in one sitting; £450 (£135,000) playing dominoes. In three years he lost £3,243 (£972,900).

His typical day started at eight in the morning, which was much later than most of his subjects, who rose at first light. He would be dressed by specially appointed "gentlemen of the privy chamber" with the support of young serving boys who warmed and fetched his clothes, but were under strict instructions neither to touch the King nor to speak to him. Henry would then be visited by his barber for a daily trim of his hair and beard. He would have a small breakfast in his private chamber, and attend a short church service followed by a large dinner at 10am. He would then mount his horse and hunt all day until about 4pm. Only very severe weather deterred him. He would return for supper in the late afternoon, and consume vast amounts of meat and wine. He would be served 13 dishes in two courses.

His favourite food was venison (deer), haggis, eels, salmon, sturgeon, beef and game pie stuffed with oranges. For pudding he liked tarts, custards, fritters, jelly and cream of almonds. The cost of each meal was equivalent to £1,285 today. Although he usually chose to eat in his private chamber he was always served with great formality. The meal would be announced by the sound of trumpets. The King would sit alone beneath a canopy and would choose friends and courtiers to stand nearby to chat with him, whilst bowing servants brought the dishes.

The evening would be spent dancing, gambling, playing cards, watching or performing in masques in which courtiers would dress in elaborate costumes and present little scenes. Henry would go to bed at about midnight. Most people, unable to afford to light their evenings with candles, would have already been asleep for several hours.

The extravagant young King was the opposite of his austere, hard-working father.

CHAPTER FIVE
Wolsey and War

What Henry was *not* doing was working. He did not attend the meetings of his Council. He could not be bothered to check the accounts of money coming in and out. He didn't like reading letters. Writing he found "somewhat tedious and painful". He employed secretaries and advisors to do all the dull business of running the country. From early on his chief advisor was Thomas Wolsey. He made Wolsey his Lord Chancellor and rewarded him with several lucrative jobs as Archbishop of York, Bishop of Winchester, Abbot of St. Albans, and more.

Wolsey, the son of an Ipswich butcher, was 20 years older than Henry. Like Henry, he loved fine food and grand living. He became famous for his huge belly and his vast wealth. His palace, Hampton Court, outshone all Henry's palaces. He employed a thousand servants. Unlike Henry, he loved to work. According to one of his attendants he could write from four in the morning until four in the afternoon, without stopping "once to piss".

Wolsey's only chance of persuading Henry to attend to the state papers came at the end of his long evenings of feasting and gambling. Henry could not be bothered to read letters written to him, let alone study long, detailed documents setting out agreements with other countries.

"Your Grace," Wolsey gently prodded, "knowing that it should be painful to visit and overread the whole treaty, I have taken the liberty of writing a short summary of the essential points. Furthermore, your Grace, there are six letters that require replies. To assist your Grace, I have again taken the liberty of writing these replies, that your Grace only needeth to provide a signature."

"Later! my loving servant, later!"

Henry laughed dismissively, and Wolsey stepped back, but stayed to watch the King carefully, waiting for a better moment to capture his attention. The King was happy to leave most decisions to Wolsey. However, if an issue suddenly caught his imagination, Henry would push aside his supper dishes and turn his full attention to it. When Henry decided to attend to business his capacity to grasp complex issues was phenomenal. He saw quickly to the heart of issues. He spotted inconsistencies. He took big decisions and, once he had taken them, he would not change his mind. As Wolsey said on his deathbed, realising that Henry had turned against him, the King could never be persuaded against "his will and appetite".

In other words, Wolsey had authority in all the areas that bored Henry, but what Henry wanted he got.

The issue which really excited Henry, and which he was always happy to attend to, was war. For Henry, war was a great glamorous adventure. All his life he dreamt of being a fighting hero like the great Henry V who had defeated the French. Henry launched his first attack on France in 1512. He would have done so earlier, but he couldn't get the agreement of the old counsellors he had inherited from his father, nor could he find an ally. He had now shaken off his father's advisors, established Wolsey as his man, and persuaded his wife's father, King Ferdinand of Spain, to join him in attacking the French.

The campaign was a fiasco. Six thousand men, an "army-by-sea", set sail for the French coast from Southhampton. They were expecting the Spanish to meet them at the coast and supply them with horses and equipment. The English troops disembarked and waited. They were miserable. It rained every day. There were not enough tents, not enough food and, worst of all, not enough beer. The soldiers complained that the local cider made them sick and the French wine was too "hot". The Spanish never turned up. In the end the English troops, disobeying Henry's orders, hired themselves ships and sailed home.

The humiliation of this sorry episode was not enough to put Henry off. He now gathered a much greater army of 40,000 men. He ordered thousands of glittering suits of armour from Spain and Italy. He commissioned a new ship, *The Great Harry,* and went daily to the docks to watch it being built. Tents, pavilions, bows and arrows, pikes and bills, and a dozen great cannons called the Twelve Apostles were loaded up. This time the army would be self-sufficient. There was food a plenty and gallons and gallons of beer. Of course, it all cost a fortune.

It was another fiasco. Again the Spanish didn't show up. Henry decided to carry on alone. One of his friends, Edward Howard, led the massive fleet to attack the Brittany coast. When a French galley ship came out to meet them, Howard boarded it, only to be pinned against its rails and chucked overboard. The remains of the leaderless fleet sloped back to Plymouth.

Henry himself joined the next attack and landed in Calais, which had long been under English control, on the 30th of June 1513. Again the fleet was magnificent. Henry wasn't one to travel lightly; he took Wolsey, 115 choristers, plus minstrels, players, trumpeters, clerks, 300 members of the household, two bishops, a duke, some lords, a vast bed, many changes of royal clothing and plenty of jewellery. They spent three weeks in Calais, partying and preparing for battle. When they finally set off to march inland they were drenched by heavy rain and only managed to travel three miles on the first day. However, both the weather and the English luck improved and by the end of the summer they had gained hold of the French town of Tournai. This was considered a great glory and was celebrated by three weeks of feasts and revels and balls and tilts and tournaments before Henry and his huge entourage set sail for home, the first royal campaign successfully completed.

Whilst Henry was busy making glorious war in

France, Katharine of Aragon had been left in charge of the country. Foolishly King James V of Scotland reckoned that this would be a good moment to invade the north of England. He seriously underestimated Katharine. She was absolutely thrilled to have a war of her own to fight.

"It will provide great sport!" she exclaimed, and excitedly wrote to Wolsey (so that he would read her letter out loud to Henry): "My heart is very good to it, and I am horribly busy with making standards, banners and badges." In fact, the Queen's involvement went much further than sewing. She co-ordinated the English military response, organising three armies, one of which she led herself, as well as a naval fleet. Her strategy was ruthless. The Scottish invaders were secretly encircled, and massacred in the dead of night. Ten thousand Scots were killed at the battle of Flodden, and one of them was their King.

Henry and Katharine had both won their battles. But the biggest battle that either of them would face was to be the battle between them.

Chapter Six
Katharine of Aragon

The first duty of a queen was to produce a son and heir. Katharine made a good start. Less than five months after their wedding, in November 1509, Henry wrote to her father Ferdinand: "Your daughter, her Serene Highness the Queen, our dearest consort, has conceived in her womb a living child and is right heavy therewith." But on the 31st of January she miscarried a daughter. Strangely, her belly continued to swell. Katharine, and her doctors, concluded that she was carrying a surviving twin. Preparations for the birth continued. Henry's cradle was re-covered in crimson cloth of gold, its pommels repainted with Katharine's coat of arms beside Henry's. Arrangements were made to employ a wet nurse (it was considered unseemly for queens to breastfeed their own babies), a nanny and two helpers to take turns rocking the cradle. Katharine's chambers were prepared for her labour. It was the tradition for English queens to retire to their chambers at the end of a pregnancy to await the birth in quiet isolation, with only their female attendants for company. They would remain in this confinement for six weeks after the birth. Their rooms were turned into a kind of cosy womb, with walls, floor and ceiling draped in tapestries, and only one window left uncovered for light. The tapestries were all of gentle abstract designs, no grisly scenes which might give the Queen nightmares and disturb her unborn child. It was in March, just as the days were lengthening, that Katharine retired to her dark chambers.

She waited for the birth. She waited and waited. She sat by the single window lacing collars for the baby's gowns. Her lady, Elizabeth Fitzwalter, stitched beside her.

"Where is my lord, the King? Why does he not visit?"

"His Majesty is jousting, my Lady."

"Why doth thou blush? Lady Elizabeth? What doth thou hide?"

"My Lady?"

"Is there no one I can trust?"

"My Lady."

The next day Lady Elizabeth Fitzwalter did not appear.

Katharine gave up the tradition of silently waiting for the King to visit and demanded to see him. Finally, Henry came. In his hunting gear, attendants in tow.

"My Lord," said Katharine calmly. Her English was excellent, but her Spanish accent remained very strong. "I wish to know why my Lady Elizabeth is no longer at court."

Henry snorted impatiently. "Your Lady Elizabeth hath offended me."

"How, my Lord?"

"She hath informed Lord Hastings that his wife, her sister Anne, doth bear me too much affection. Lord Hastings hath forthwith banished my Lady Anne to a convent."

"But, My Lord, I trust you bear no special affection to Lady Anne. I trust you bear no love to any woman, save myself, your wife, only."

Henry raised his eyes to the tapestried ceiling. He didn't reply. He didn't need to.

The whole court soon learnt of the rift between the King and Queen. Katharine stayed hidden in the dark chambers, even though her swollen belly was subsiding, even though she could no longer hide from the depressing truth that there was no baby. Her large belly may have been caused by infection; perhaps she had simply put on weight. At last she could pretend no longer. On the 27th of May, four months after the miscarriage, she wrote to her father to tell him that her child had been stillborn. She added, rather unnecessarily, that this "is considered to be a misfortune in England".

She did not, yet, tell him the good news that she was pregnant again. The King and Queen had recently been reconciled. The second pregnancy went smoothly and on New Year's Day 1511, at 1.30 am, Katharine, in her tapestried chamber, gave birth to a son.

The birth was announced by round after round of gunfire from the Tower of London. Celebratory parades filled the streets. The fountains flowed with wine. When he was five days old, the baby was christened Henry. He was then handed over to his wet nurse. His father Henry immediately went on a pilgrimage of thanksgiving to Walsingham in Norfolk, before hosting the greatest tournament of his reign. The event was recorded on a 60-foot-long roll of vellum, which shows a series of scenes in bold colours and gold leaf. Henry jousts before Katharine. He is breaking his lance upon his opponent's helmet. His horse wears a blue velvet cloth decorated with golden "K"s for Katharine, and golden hearts. Golden letters spell the word "loyall". The Queen sits beneath a golden canopy, applauding with joy.

It was their happiest moment. Ten days later, baby Henry was dead.

Katharine was to have four more pregnancies. Three of these babies died. But one child was a healthy, full-term baby who survived. Unfortunately she was a girl. They christened her Mary.

The following year Henry did in fact have a son, also called Henry, but his mother was not Queen Katharine; she was a lady of the court called Elizabeth Blount. So, with a legitimate daughter and an illegitimate son, Henry still had no male heir, and Katharine seemed unlikely ever to produce one.

CHAPTER SEVEN
Cloth of Gold

In 1519 Europe was in the hands of three young glory-seeking men: Henry, now 28; Francois I, King of France, aged 25; and Katharine of Aragon's nephew, Charles, King of Aragon, who was only 19, and had just been elected Holy Roman Emperor, which made him ruler of almost all the rest of Europe. A power struggle was inevitable.

Of the three young kings, Henry had the smallest empire. But he hoped that he could prove that he was the most spectacular ruler by dazzling the other kings with lavish entertainments. He began with Katharine's nephew Charles, now known as Charles V, who agreed to a brief trip to England in the spring of 1520. The King of Aragon had a terrible journey, his fleet of ships stranded for six weeks by strong winds blowing in the wrong direction. He finally landed in Dover, and was taken by Wolsey to Dover Castle, where he was planning to rest before travelling on to Canterbury to meet Henry and Katharine the following day. The young King was fast asleep in bed when Henry, who loved to surprise his guests, and had galloped over from Cantebury, bounced up the castle stairs. A startled Charles emerged from his bedroom, and was soon smothered in a great bear hug from the English King. Four days of banqueting and Spanish dancing followed before the Holy Roman Emperor sailed on.

Francois I, King of France, was not prepared to travel to England. He wanted to entertain Henry on his own land. There were endless negotiations until it was finally agreed that Henry and Francois would meet exactly on the *border* of their lands. Henry had inherited some French land, including Calais, and there it was he arrived on the 31st of May 1520 with a fleet of 27 ships, carrying 3,997 people and 2,087 horses. Katharine sailed separately, accompanied by a further 1,175 people and 778 horses. The first meeting of the two Kings was carefully choreographed so that they both approached the border of their lands at the same moment. In synchrony, they left behind their escorts and galloped forward to greet each other. Reaching the border they embraced three times on horseback. This cannot have been easy, for both sides secretly feared an attack and both Kings were in battle gear. Pretty fancy battle gear: each wore cloth of gold encrusted with jewels. Finally, they dismounted and embraced again before retiring to drink spiced wine in Francois' gold damask pavillion.

Henry stayed for 17 days. Each day was finely tuned so that the two Kings took exactly equal turns at playing host and guest. But there were tensions. After watching a wrestling match, an excited Henry challenged the French King to a round. He was, to his embarrassment, quickly thrown to the ground. Tactfully, Francois suggested an archery contest, in which Henry was conveniently victorious.

For the purpose of entertaining the French, Henry built a stone and timber palace. It was enormous. Three of its rooms were bigger than any hall in any palace in the whole of England. Their vast walls were draped in cloth of gold. The floors were covered in Turkish carpets. At a time when glass windows were a rare luxury, vast windows were glazed with diamond shaped panes. The extravagance was stupendous.

Beyond the palace were 2,800 tents also adorned

with gold cloth, giving the place its name the "Field of Cloth of Gold". A golden fountain flowed with white wine, Malmsey wine and claret. Not surprisingly, there were soon complaints about the heaps of drunks who lay around snoring. And of course, there was food in abundance: 2,000 sheep, 1,300 chickens, 800 calves, 340 beef cattle, 314 heron, 13 swans, 17 deer, 9,000 plaice, 7,000 whiting, 700 conger eels, 4 bushels of mustard, gallons of cream, and vast quantities of sugar which was used to build enormous sugar statues. Never had the world seen such an extravagant display. It was supposed to cement the friendship of the Kings. They parted with gifts of jewels and horses. But it was all false. France continued to be England's worst enemy. Three years later they were at war again.

CHAPTER EIGHT
Ann Boleyn

By 1525 it was clear to everyone at court that Henry had lost interest in his Queen. He had had several affairs. Katharine was six years older than Henry, and her body had been exhausted by the endless pregnancies. Francois I, King of France, famously described her as "an old deformed wife… while (Henry) himself is young and handsome."

By deformed, he meant fat. Katharine was always very short and by the age of 35 she is said to have been as wide as she was tall. She and Henry led increasingly separate lives. As Henry continued to hunt and joust and dance, Katharine withdrew from the court festivities and turned her attention to bringing up her daughter, Mary – in whom Henry seemed to have no interest – and to God.

Henry was 34 when something happened to him which had probably never happened before, and was never to happen so powerfully again. He fell in love; passionately, hopelessly in love. The object of his love was a woman called Anne Boleyn.

Anne seems to have been one of those people who provoke strong feelings in others. Lots of men fell in love with her. Lots of people hated her. Henry, tragically, was to do both. When Henry first noticed her, she was in her early twenties. She was the sister of his mistress Mary Boleyn, and a lady-in-waiting to his wife Katharine. Her father Thomas and brother George were courtiers. Mary had just given birth to a boy, whom she called Henry. He could have been the son of either Henry or her husband, William Carey, but Henry never acknowledged him as his own. The King always seemed to lose interest in women when they had babies and, on this occasion, bored by the pregnant Mary, he turned his attention to her sister.

Anne was not famed for her beauty, but it is clear from her portraits that she was striking. In Tudor portraits no one ever smiles, and this makes most people – Katharine of Aragon, for example – look very solemn. But Anne, even without a smile, looks vibrant.

Her eyes are full of light, and hold one's gaze directly. Her lips are clear and firm. Her neck long and elegant. Five hundred years have not dimmed the sense that she is a power to be reckoned with.

When Henry fell in love with Anne, she did something no woman had yet done to him. She rejected him. It was a brave thing to do, and very clever. For her refusal entranced him. He *had* to have her. He pestered her, he followed her, he begged for secret assignations. In the end, she agreed to meet him in her brother's chambers. In the evening, returning from the hunt, Henry came to find her. Without stopping to take off his muddy clothes or to wash his sweaty body he came for her. She was waiting, but not willing. Her cool, pure calm stopped him in his tracks. The great monarch went down on his knees.

"Madam, I am your loyal and most assured servant. I have put myself in great distress, not knowing if I have your affection. I beseech you to give yourself up, body and soul, to me, and I will take you for my only mistress, rejecting from thought and affection all others save yourself, to serve you only."

Anne kept her distance. "I think Your Majesty speaks these words in mirth. I beseech Your Highness most earnestly to desist. I would rather lose my life than my honesty."

"Well, Madam. I shall live in hope."

"I understand not, most mighty King, how you should keep such hope! Your wife I cannot be, because you have a Queen already. Your mistress I will not be."

Anne knew, from Mary's experience, that Henry soon tired of his mistresses and abandoned them. She wanted nothing less than to be his Queen. Henry kept hoping that Anne would not change her mind, and give in to him. His demands became more and more pressing. So Anne decided to take herself right away from the court, and withdraw to her parents' home, Hever Castle.

If Anne secretly hoped that her absence would make Henry's heart grow even fonder, she was right. Henry, the man who hated writing, beseiged her with love letters, doodling his signature with hearts, "written with the hand of him that longeth to be yours". His letters show that Anne had not been completely cold to him. "Oft and again I wisheth you in your brother's room... wishing myself (specially an evening) in my sweetheart's arms, whose pretty dukkys [breasts] I trust shortly to kiss."

Nonetheless, Anne continued to refuse to live as his wife without being officially married. And at last Henry resolved that there was only one way in which he could satisfy his two greatest desires: his desire for Anne and his desire for a legitimate son and heir. He had to divorce Katharine so that he could marry Anne, and then she could bear him a son.

CHAPTER NINE
Divorce

Five hundred years ago divorce wasn't what it is today. In fact there wasn't really any such thing. You couldn't end a marriage just because it had problems. Violence, cruelty, abandonment; none of these were considered reasons for ending a marriage. The only way to get out of a marriage was to prove that it had never actually been a proper marriage. The person you had to convince was the Pope, who was head of the church in Rome.

So this is what Henry set out to do: to persuade the Pope that his marriage to Katharine of Aragon had never been a proper marriage. It wasn't an easy task. For a start Katharine and Henry had been married the best part of 20 years before it occurred to him to question it. Furthermore, Henry had decided to argue that the marriage was illegal because Katharine had previously been married to his brother. And yet Henry and Katharine had been given special permission by the Pope to marry in the first place.

Unfortunately, at the moment that Henry decided he wanted a divorce from Katharine of Aragon, the Pope was a prisoner of Katharine's nephew Charles V and he was unable to make any decisions without Charles V's agreement. Charles, the Holy Roman Emperor, was far too powerful for Henry to challenge. He would never agree to his aunt Katharine losing her position as Queen of England.

In these impossible circumstances, Wolsey was given the job of trying to win the Pope's backing for the divorce. Rather unconvincingly, Henry was claiming that, much as he would love to stay married to Katharine, he had now realised that the marriage was unlawful, and he felt it was his duty to divorce her. There were endless letters and arguments and diplomatic missions. But, unsurprisingly, there was no progress. What *was* progressing was Henry's relationship with Anne. She still refused to be his mistress, but from May 1527 she accepted the role of unofficial First Lady, appearing in public with Henry in the place of

Katharine of Aragon. Katharine meanwhile was ordered to live in exile from the court, in a series of remote, damp houses. Henry humiliated her by ordering her to return the jewels he had given her, so that he could give them to Anne. Most cruel of all, Henry commanded that Katharine could not see their daughter Mary. It was not a custody battle. Henry did not want to live with Mary himself. Rather, he avoided seeing her, and insisted that the divorce would mean that Mary was to be considered illegitimate, no longer his lawful daughter, no longer heir to his throne.

Anne was now impatient to become Queen and convinced that Wolsey was not doing all he could to advance what she and Henry called "Our Great Matter". Anne and Wolsey had never got on well. A few years earlier, Wolsey had prevented her from marrying a young man in his household called Henry Percy. This was probably on Henry's instructions, for it was about the time that Henry had first noticed Anne. Wolsey apparently separated Anne and Percy on the grounds that she was socially inferior. Percy, who adored Anne, had cried and cried and refused to abandon her but, threatened with disinheritance he had reluctantly returned home to Northumberland and made a miserable marriage to somebody else. Percy was heartbroken, and perhaps Anne was too. She certainly held the view that Wolsey was her enemy.

From the moment Henry fell in love with Anne, she and Wolsey were in competition with each other for the King's trust. Neither Katharine of Aragon nor any of Henry's mistresses had ever threatened Wolsey's position as Henry's chief advisor, the most powerful person in the kingdom. But Anne was different and when Anne and Wolsey disagreed about the best tactics for getting the divorce, Henry listened to Anne.

In the summer of 1527 Wolsey was on a very grand mission to the French royal court, supposedly negotiating an "Eternal Peace". Henry and Anne were on their annual summer holiday which involved roving from one great country house to the next, stopping at each for a spot of hunting. On the 23rd of July they arrived at New Hall, an Essex mansion which had previously belonged to the Boleyn family. Here they were joined by the Dukes of Norfolk and Suffolk, the Marquess of Exeter, the Earls of Essex, Oxford and Rutland, Viscount Fitzwalter, and Anne's brother Viscount Rochford. It was Henry's grand inner circle, which included several of Anne's relatives. The party lasted more than a month. There was the usual hunting and feasting, but more importantly there was talk. It was during this houseparty that a new divorce strategy was hatched. The scheme was Anne's. Wolsey was 250 miles away, and in his absence he was replaced as chief negotiator by a young secretary called William Knight.

Wolsey rushed back from France. He rode straight to the Palace of Richmond where Henry and Anne now were. On arrival he demanded, "When should I repair to the King's Privy Chamber?" He was expecting a private meeting with Henry. But the servant returned with a message from Anne: "Tell him that he may come here, where the King is." There was no question of a meeting without her present.

Anne may not yet have been Queen, but she was behaving as if she had the authority of a queen. From now on, Wolsey was increasingly humiliated. He lost his job as Lord Chancellor. He had to give up several of his lucrative positions in the church. He was forced to give Henry his grand palace Hampton Court, as well as his London residence of York Place. He was banished to Esher in Surrey, without "beds, sheets, table cloths, cups and dishes" which he had to borrow from friends. He later moved to Richmond, and then York.

Wolsey complained to friends about the influence of Anne, "the night crow", who "called continually upon the King in his ear". Even more dangerously, he continued to communicate with the Pope, sending secret coded letters, without Henry's authority. The suspicion was that he was looking for support abroad in his battle with Anne, trying to get the Pope to insist that Henry and Anne separate. On the 1st of November 1530, Henry issued a warrant for Wolsey's arrest. The person sent to York to arrest him was none other than Anne's former love, Henry Percy, now Earl of Northumberland who, "trembling" and "with a very faint and soft voice", declared, "I arrest you of High Treason."

Wolsey never made it to his trial. On his journey from York to the Tower of London, he was held under house arrest for two weeks at Sheffield Park, home of the Earl of Shrewsbury. Here, one evening, after a dinner which ended with baked pears for pudding, he became suddenly ill with agonizing stomach cramps. An apothecary was sent for, and Wolsey was given a remedy which made him "break wind upward". This eased his pain, but he soon developed acute diarrhoea. When Sir William Kingston, the Keeper of the Tower of London, arrived to escort Wolsey to prison, the cardinal was too ill to be moved. He lay pale and exhausted. His vast body was shrunken by his illness.

"I will die tomorrow," he insisted. "It is God, and not the King that I must answer to. And God knows that I am innocent of all these malicious accusations." His mind was completely clear, and his thoughts were with the King.

"He is a prince of royal courage, and hath a princely heart... I have often kneeled before him in his private chamber on my knees for the space of an hour or two, to persuade him from his will and appetite; but I could never dissuade him therefrom... I warn you to be well advised and assured what matter you put in his head; for you shall never pull it out again."

Despite his weakness, Wolsey made his attendants raise him to his knees upon the bed so that he could pray. His final words were a prayer that he be damned "if ever I thought to do a disservice to my King." Laying back down, he slipped into unconsciousness and died.

The rumour was that he had been poisoned.

Anne had won the battle for influence over Henry, but Katharine of Aragon was still the Queen. The new divorce strategy was for Henry to set himself up as Supreme Head of the Church of England, with full powers to grant divorces. He would then be able to grant one to himself. So he set up a special commission to look into whether he as King of England was the rightful head of the church, or whether the Pope was the rightful head. And guess what? The commission found that Henry was by rights the "Supreme Head on Earth of the Church of England". He promptly appointed a new Archbishop of Canterbury, a friend of Anne Boleyn's called Thomas Cranmer, and under these newly discovered powers Archbishop Cranmer declared on the 23rd of May 1533 that the marriage of Henry and Katharine was null and void. Henry was free to marry again.

In the end, Henry and Anne had not waited until he was divorced. They had married secretly in the autumn of 1532 and Anne had soon become pregnant. The marriage was bigamous and illegal. So as soon as they had realised that she was pregnant, they had married for a second time, in January 1533. In fact, this marriage was also bigamous, illegal, and supposedly secret, but news of it was deliberately leaked to the public, so that no one would be shocked by the sight of Anne's growing belly. When Archbishop Cranmer granted Henry's divorce from Katharine, he declared that the marriage to Anne was legal. All these shenanigans were designed to make sure that the child that Anne was carrying was accepted as the legitimate heir to the throne. Henry had been assured by Anne's doctors and by astrologers that it was a boy.

When Anne was crowned Queen, in June 1533, she was six months pregnant. She went into her confined chambers in late August. The royal clerks wrote out birth announcements for "a prince". Plans were made for celebratory jousts. Sooner than expected, on the afternoon of the 7th of September, Anne gave birth.

It was a girl. An extra "s" was added to the birth announcements to turn the male "Prince" into female "Princes" (spelling not being what it is today). Three days later the baby was christened Elizabeth. The jousts were cancelled. A daughter was nothing to celebrate.

Anne and Henry had had their first public row just before she retired for her confinement. She had seen Henry flirting with another woman. Henry was unashamed. He told her "that she must shut her eyes and endure as her betters had done." With pregnancy she had lost her power over him, and unless she quickly produced a son she knew that she would lose him altogether.

Two years after Henry and Anne married, Katharine died. Like Wolsey she had terrible pains in her stomach and again there were rumours of poisoning. When news of her death reached Henry he was delighted. He dressed from top to toe in yellow, except for a white feather in his bonnet. He went to church with a fanfare of trumpets, showing off the baby Elizabeth who was all dolled up in royal finery. After the church service he sat down to a great feast and then made his way to Anne's apartments. He called for Elizabeth to be brought again, and he pranced around with her, showing her off to each of Anne's ladies in turn. Then he summoned the musicians, and kissed each of Anne's ladies, cuddled them and swung them in a wild dance around the room. Anne watched quietly. She was pregnant again, but there were vague pains in her belly. When at last the King stopped dancing, she retired to bed alone. What if this baby was not a son? Would he do to her what he had done to Katharine?

In fact, of course, her fate was to be much worse.

CHAPTER TEN.
Religion and Rebellion

During Henry's reign many people throughout Europe were turning against the authority of the Pope. Because they protested against the Catholic Church they were called Protestants. Although Henry rejected the Pope, he had no time for these Protestants. They claimed that all people were equal in the eyes of God. This was not Henry's view at all. He claimed to be closer to God than anyone else in his kingdom.

In 1534 a Statute of Parliament declared that Henry was second only to Jesus Christ. Henry insisted that all the parish priests in the country cross out every mention of the Pope in every prayer book in every church. Every single person over the age of 14 had to be prepared to swear on oath that Henry was Supreme

Head of the Church, and that his marriage to Anne was legal (this was before Henry himself decided that the marriage wasn't legal, of course). Refusal to swear this oath was High Treason to be punished by hanging, drawing and quartering.

The killings began in May 1535, when four monks and one priest were sentenced to death for denying Henry's title as "Supreme Head of the Church in England". One by one, so that they were forced to watch the deaths of their fellow victims, these men were hanged, cut down whilst still alive, and castrated. Their bellies were then slit open and their intestines and bowels cut out. Still alive they then had to watch as their innards were burnt in front of them. Only then were they finally beheaded, and quartered.

Further killings followed. Sir Thomas More, who had been Henry's Lord Chancellor, and John Fisher, Cardinal of Rochester, both refused the oath. As men of high status they were spared the horrors of the hanging, drawing and quartering and were simply beheaded.

As Supreme Head of the Church of England, Henry not only gained control of the church, he also gained access to its wealth. In order to get his hands on the money he decided to undertake a massive programme of asset stripping. This meant closing down parts of the

church and taking
everything of value
for himself: buildings,
land, precious orna-
ments etc. For this
project he needed a
ruthless henchman;
and he found one in
Thomas Cromwell.

Cromwell had
worked for Wolsey and like Wolsey he was not from a
grand family, but he was extraordinarily hardworking
and a very effective administrator. Henry, who was
now massive, treated him roughly: "He hath been well
pummelled about the head and shaken up as it were a
dog." Unlike Wolsey, Cromwell was not a priest, so it
was very surprising when Henry appointed him to be
Vicar-General. This gave him authority over all the
bishops and archbishops, and made him second only to
Henry as Head of the Church. That was third after
Jesus Christ.

Cromwell's mission as Vicar-General was to destroy
the monasteries and nunneries. The monasteries were
old established religious institutions which trained
priests, whilst the nunneries were the equivalent for

women. And they were not terribly popular. They were supposed to be places where monks or nuns could lead good and pure lives, providing education and care for the sick and the poor. Very often, however, they had lost sight of these ideals. In some cases, it was said, that instead of providing housing for the homeless, they behaved like ruthless landlords, extorting high rents. There were often rumours that monks and nuns were leading immoral lives.

Many people believed that these religious houses needed reforming and improving. And Henry pretended that this was what he wanted to do when he instructed Cromwell to send a team of inspectors around all the monasteries and nunneries, and to close every institution which was found to be corrupt. In reality his interest was not in improving the monasteries, but in grabbing their money. All the wealth of every monastery or nunnery that was closed down went straight to Henry.

Cromwell dispatched his inspectors. They were looking for trouble and sometimes it was easy to find. When they arrived unannounced at Langdon Abbey in Kent, for example, they caught the Abbot canoodling with a woman in a garden shed. The embarrassed Abbot refused to open the shed door so the inspectors broke it down with an axe. The woman and the Abbot were both imprisoned. Sometimes vice was harder to detect. The worst the inspectors could pin on the Abbot of Shrewsbury was that he had failed to mend a leak in the chapel roof. In the end, Henry managed to close down three-quarters of the monastic houses – all but the largest and most powerful. These he saved for later.

Chapter Eleven
The Fall of Anne Boleyn

A couple of weeks after Katharine's death in January 1536, Henry, now hugely fat, was preparing for a jousting tournament when he and his great horse, "fell so heavily that everyone thought it a miracle he was not killed". He was unconscious for two hours, but otherwise unhurt.

Five days later, January 29, Katharine was buried in Peterborough. Neither Henry nor Anne attended. They were in Greenwich Palace. In the morning Henry attended a solemn service in the chapel. In the afternoon, Anne, who had not seen her husband all day, found him in one of the private chambers with her lady-in-waiting Jane Seymour on his knee. Anne screamed. She screamed and screamed. Jane ran from the room. Henry tried to soothe his wife. "Peace be sweetheart, remember our child." He was afraid that her hysteria would harm the baby she was carrying, and he was right. Within hours Anne was gripped by pain, and that evening she miscarried a 15-week-old foetus. It was the longed-for boy.

Henry had no words of comfort for her. "It is clear that God does not wish me to have a male child."

"Oh my lord," sobbed Anne. "I promise we will have a son. I can carry a baby. I only lost this baby because of my great sorrow. I had such fear when I heard news of your fall at the jousts. And my heart broke when I saw that you loved another."

Henry was unmoved. He did now love another and all his passion for Anne had turned to hatred. All the miscarriages of his two wives and the failure to produce a healthy and legitimate son, were a great humiliation to him. His manhood was being called into question. The failure had to be Anne's, not his. He declared that she was a witch, and their marriage was illegal, for she had seduced him into it by witchcraft. He installed Jane Seymour's brother Edward and his wife into rooms which connected with his private chambers through a secret passageway. With Edward Seymore keen for a royal connection to be established with his family,

Henry could now see Jane alone whenever he wished.

Henry wanted to be rid of Anne, and quickly. He wanted to marry Jane and have a son with her. Behind the scenes Anne's downfall was being plotted. It started with rumours that Anne was flirting with a number of courtiers. The night before the annual May Day jousting tournament, Mark Smeaton, said to be the king's favourite young musician, was suddenly arrested for questioning. He was accused of having an affair with Anne. The May Day jousts went ahead as planned: there were bright banners, trumpets, and knights in shining armour charging on great horses. Anne smiled and waved from her golden-clothed viewing box. Henry was glowing and gallant, lending his own charger to a courtier called Henry Norris whose horse was playing up. It was the last time the King and Queen would ever see each other. When the jousting finished, Henry disappeared without a word.

That evening Mark Smeaton, desperately pleading his innocence, was taken to the Tower. He was sent straight down to the cold, stone dungeons and into the torture chamber. Here was the dreaded rack: a large machine with cogs which enabled it to extend, and pull apart the body of the victim. Smeaton's arms and legs were bound to the rack. At first there would be a feeling of lengthening and tightening, but within minutes the pain was excruciating. Each arm and leg dislocated from its socket, and still they were pulled. Most people would confess to anything to avoid the torture of the rack. It was known to leave its victims unable to use their limbs ever again. Mark Smeaton was extraordinary. He bore the pain for four hours. And then he confessed. He told the torturers what he knew they wanted to hear. That he had committed adultery with the Queen. The confession got him off the rack, but he knew it would lead to certain execution.

At dawn the next morning another courtier, Henry Norris, who had borrowed the King's horse only hours earlier, was taken to the Tower. Norris had for many years held the post of Groom of the Stool, a position of great honour, which gave him responsibility for emptying the King's chamber pot and wiping the King's bottom. He too was accused of adultery with the Queen.

The following day Anne herself was arrested. She was interrogated by a council which included her uncle, the Duke of Norfolk. He was no doubt fearful of accusations that as Anne's relative he was on her side. So, to protect himself, he made a great show of shaking his head in disgust at the accusations that she had had relationships with several courtiers, and on three or four occasions he said, "Tut, tut, tut" loudly. That night Anne was taken by boat to the Tower. She was hysterical, crying wildly and then falling "into a great laughing" over and over again.

A few hours later Anne's brother, George, Viscount Rochford, was brought to the Tower and interrogated. Not only was Anne accused of numerous affairs, but also of incest committed with her brother.

In the past Anne had shown enormous self-control. But now she was panicking. She couldn't think straight. She kept talking and talking, trying to make sense of what had happened. If only she could find an explanation, if she could understand why the King thought that she could possibly have been unfaithful to him, then she would be able to explain to him what a terrible misunderstanding there had been. Over and over again she went through all the recent conversations she had had.

She would have done better to keep quiet. She remembered a conversation with Sir Francis Weston, a former page boy of Henry's. She had once seen him paying attention to a lady of the court who was not his wife, she said, and she had challenged him "that he did love her kinswoman Mrs. Shelton and that … he loved not his wife." According to Anne, Weston had replied obsequiously that "he loved one in her house better than them both." "Who is that?" Anne had asked. "It is yourself," he said. Within hours of Anne recalling this, Weston was also in the Tower, and soon beheaded.

More and more courtiers were arrested. Henry was determined to destroy Anne. By the end of the first week of May, Sir Richard Page, Sir Thomas Wyatt, Sir Francis Bryan and William Brereton were all in the Tower, accused of improper relations with the Queen.

The first trials were held on the 12th May. Smeaton, who would have been returned to the rack if he changed his plea, continued to plead guilty. Norris, Weston and Brereton pleaded not guilty. All four were found guilty.

The trial of Anne and her brother was held three days later. Two thousand spectators crowded excitedly into the Great Hall in the Tower of London. The King himself did not attend. It fell to the Duke of Norfolk, uncle to both the accused, to be the presiding judge, the Lord High Sheriff for the day. He sat on a high throne, as the King's representative, wearing an ermine cape and the great chains of office around his neck. His long, thin face was pale with the strain of the betrayal he was making to his niece and nephew. Sitting in judgement with him were 26 lords of the realm. Henry used a favourite trick of violent leaders. He forced the people whom he feared might object to Anne's execution to take part in her trial, so that they would share the responsibility for her death, and could not protest about it with a clear conscience. For this reason Henry Percy, now the Earl of Northumberland, who had so loved Anne, was also on the panel of judges. He was shivering with nerves and illness, his stomach aching with grief. All the judges knew that, if they refused to provide Henry with the guilty verdict he wanted, they could be accused of High Treason themselves, and executed.

The crowd fell silent as Anne calmly entered the Hall. She curtsied to the judges, and was then led to a seat on a central platform to hear the charges: "Queen Anne, you are charged with the crime of cohabiting with your brother, Lord Rochford, and with other accomplices; with promising Henry Norris that you would marry him after the death of the King; with poisoning Katharine, Dowager Princess of Wales; with intriguing to poison Princess Mary."

"My Lord," replied Anne, bowing her head to her uncle, "I am not guilty of any of the charges. I have not cohabited with any man, save my Lord the King. I admit only to natural kinship with my brother, and to friendship with gentlemen of the court. In gratitude for their service, I have often found occasion to give gifts to the courtiers, as is natural for a Queen. I have always been faithful to the King. I have never plotted to poison anyone."

"My Lords," said Norfolk, turning to the 26 peers, "What is your verdict?"

"Guilty."

"Guilty."

"Guilty."

Each peer in turn, staring at the floor, pronounced the same, the inevitable verdict.

Norfolk turned to face his niece. He struggled to keep his voice steady as he pronounced the sentence: "Because thou hast offended our sovereign lord the King's Grace in committing treason against his person, the law of the realm is this: that thou shall be burnt here within the Tower of London on the Green, else to have thy head smitten off, as the King's pleasure shall be further known..."

There was a shriek of agony from the crowd. Anne's old nurse, Mistress Orchard, became hysterical. Henry Percy, the Earl of Northumberland, who had just condemned to death the woman he most loved in the world, fainted, and was carried from the court. But Anne stood still and calm.

"I confess that I have had jealous fancies and suspicions of my King. But God knows, and is my witness, that I have not sinned against him in any other way."

Once Anne was condemned, her brother Rochford's trial was a foregone conclusion. He approached it boldly. One of the accusations was that Anne had said that Henry "was no good in bed with women, and that he had neither potency nor force." Rochford had been warned not to mention this, but he announced it to all 2,000 onlookers.

All the men were beheaded on the 17th of May. The scaffold was built especially high to give a good view to the vast crowds that came to watch. Henry showed some kind of mercy by excusing all these prisoners the punishment of being hanged, drawn and quartered. It is thought that Henry spared them the worst death because he knew them personally. He also spared Anne the horror of a slow death burning at the stake. Her head was to be smitten off, and Henry wanted only the best for his former Queen, so he summoned the best executioner in the world: a Frenchman, who used a sword rather than an axe.

Anne's execution was delayed for two days to give Henry time to legally divorce her before she died. This made their daughter, Elizabeth, illegitimate, which meant that, in theory, she could never become Queen. When the time finally came they were further delays. Executions traditionally took place at dawn. Knowing this, Anne rose at two in the morning to pray. Dawn broke, but there was no summons. Anne became increasingly agitated. Would Henry visit? Would he grant her a pardon at the last minute? At nine in the morning she was told that the executioner was delayed on his journey, and would not be there until midday. At midday there was still no sign of the executioner and Anne was told that she must endure another night of waiting. Her execution would now take place the following morning.

At last, at nine o'clock in the morning on Friday the 15th of May 1536, Anne was led to the scaffold. She kept looking behind her, looking for Henry, hoping for a last-minute pardon, but he was not there. Standing before the executioner, Anne made a final speech. Her words were extraordinary: "I pray God save the King, and send him long to reign over you, for never was there a gentler or more merciful Prince; and to me he was ever a good, a gentle and sovereign Lord." Her royal ermine fur mantle was then removed from her neck. She took off her headdress herself. She knelt down and tucked her dress tightly under her feet. One of her attendants then blindfolded her. The execution-er lived up to his reputation: Anne's head was cut off with a single swipe.

Chapter Twelve
Jane Seymour

From the moment Anne was arrested until the day she was executed, Henry partied furiously. He had decided that Anne was guilty. He didn't want to think about her for another minute. He didn't want to see her trial or her execution. Night after night he drank and feasted and danced; but he did not allow himself the comfort of his new woman. Jane Seymore was sent away from the court so that Henry could not be seen dallying whilst his wife was on trial for adultery. However, the minute he heard that Anne's head was off, he took a barge up the Thames to Chelsea to join Jane. The next day they were engaged, and ten days later they were married.

Jane Seymour had been one of Anne's ladies-in-waiting, and had previously served Katharine of Aragon. Her portrait by the famous Dutch painter Holbein shows a tense woman with a tight mouth, receding chin and uncomfortably clasped hands. According to one contemporary, "She is of middle height, and nobody thinks she has much beauty. Her complexion is so whitish that she may be called rather pale." After the dangerous charisma of Anne, it was Jane's very ordinariness that attracted Henry. She looked, and probably was, dull. She was quiet and undemanding. Henry fell in love with her during Anne's short, final pregnancy.

Jane herself was soon pregnant. In the spring of 1537, bonfires were lit throughout the land in celebration of the news, and prayers were said for the safe arrival of the longed-for Prince. In September, Jane entered the confined apartments where she waited quietly for three weeks for the child to be born. When the labour finally came it was long and difficult. At last, at two in the morning on Friday the 12th of October, the baby was born. It was healthy. It was a boy.

The bells of every parish church in London rang from eight that morning until ten o'clock that night. There were bonfires in the streets. There was a two-thousand-gun salute from the Tower of London. Three days later, the baby was christened Edward and proclaimed as "son and heir to the King of England" and given the titles "Duke of Cornwall and Earl of Chester".

Five days later prayers were being given for the health of Jane. She may have delivered the baby by Caesarian section, which, in Tudor times, was a matter of being cut open without anaesthetic. She was certainly weak after the birth and soon became feverish. She had caught an infection, and died at midnight on the 24th of October. The baby was 12 days old. Henry, who always tried to distract himself from pain, went straight off on a hunting expedition. But he was devastated. He loved Jane for giving him a son, and this time there was no new love to comfort him. Henry did not marry again for two years – the longest stretch of his adult life in which he remained unmarried. When Henry died, ten years later, he was buried beside Jane Seymour.

Chapter Thirteen
Pilgrimage of Grace

Throughout Henry's short marriage to Jane Seymour, his henchman, Thomas Cromwell, had carried on the programme of closing down the monasteries and grabbing all their land and money. Closing the monasteries meant closing all the schools and hospitals and care for the poor which they provided. There were bound to be protests. When Cromwell's commissioners arrived at Hexham Abbey in Northumberland on the 28th of September 1536, they found the Abbey locked and barricaded and the streets of Hexham barred by armed men. A monk wearing armour stood on the Abbey roof and declared that there were 20 monks, armed with guns and cannon, who would fight to the death to defend the Abbey. The commissioners retreated, but when Henry heard of the incident he insisted that the Abbey be stormed by force, and the monks be treated as traitors for their disobedience. This was a threat to hang, draw and quarter them if they were captured.

News of the rebellion spread quickly. Within days, 30,000 were marching on the city of Lincoln; 40,000 gathered in York. Henry, hundreds of miles away in Windsor Castle, was apoplectic with rage. He summoned all the noblemen of the court and ordered them to prepare for war. His voice, higher pitched than might be expected from of a man of his increasing size, almost shrieked: "These are traitorous, rude and ignorant common people! It is a detestable and unnatural rebellion. We will destroy, burn and kill man, woman and child, to the terrible example of all others! I promise you their utter destruction."

Henry's noble lords dutifully gathered armies and set off for the north of England to wreak the King's bloody revenge. In Cumberland hundreds of villagers and monks were hanged from the trees in their gardens until their bodies rotted – their relatives were forbidden to cut them down and bury them, so that their stinking corpses would serve as a warning to all. But still the rebellion spread. The people saw themselves as religious heroes, defending their monasteries and churches. They even gave their rebellion a religious name: "The Pilgrimage of Grace". Seeing that they could not easily be crushed by violence, Henry decided on a more devious tactic. He wrote to the rebel leader, a Yorkshireman called Robert Aske, and invited him to come and stay for Christmas. Henry, who in private always referred to him as "that villain Aske", claimed that he wanted Aske to explain to him exactly what the people of Yorkshire wanted. Aske was a good man, and a trusting man. He accepted the King's invitation.

That year there was a white Christmas. The River Thames froze. Greenwich Palace could not be reached by barge, so the King and Queen and all their guests arrived on horseback. The huge chilly rooms blazed with fires and candles. They feasted on roast meat and drank fine wine. Jugglers, jesters, muscians, entertained them. Henry danced and laughed.

"My good Friends, my own sweet darling wife, I have never been merrier. Bring the gifts. I have gifts for everyone. For you, my good friend Aske, a jacket of crimson satin! And when you wear this jacket, remember my promises. For I give you my solemn word that we will meet again in York this summer. Much I regret that I have never journied to that fair part of my kingdom. But this summer, we will crown Queen Jane in the great cathedral at York, and we will hold a parliament in that fine city, so that the people there may know us and love us! And we will pardon the rebels, they are good men, as you say, but misled by ignorance!"

Aske was delighted with the King's promises. When he returned home, he quickly spread the good news of Henry's pardon. At first the rebels were hard to convince, but Aske was so sure of the King's genuine regrets that by February most of the rebels accepted them. A small band, however, remained hostile to the King, and when they launched a new protest Henry found the excuse he was waiting for. He sent in another army. The rebels were quickly crushed. Then he turned on Aske and the original rebels.

Aske begged to be spared the dreaded hanging, drawing, quartering, "Let me be full dead ere I be dismembered." He must have regretted this plea. Henry, who always enjoyed arranging special details of executions, had Aske hanged in chains from York Castle. With no rope around his neck, it took him a week to die. And, of course, Henry didn't keep his promises. He never visited York. No parliament was held there. And Jane was never crowned.

CHAPTER FOURTEEN
Anne of Cleves

After Jane's death Henry was expected to marry again. This time Thomas Cromwell saw the opportunity for Henry to marry a foreign princess, someone who could help England make a useful alliance abroad. So Cromwell set about searching for a nice European princess. It wasn't easy. The young princesses of Europe were not impressed by Henry's track record: one divorced, one beheaded, one died. He was also getting grossly fat, and had begun to develop smelly leg ulcers. As Cromwell made approaches, the rejections poured in. The 16-year-old Dowager Duchess Christina of Milan politely declined the honour, insisting that she would happily marry Henry, if only she had two heads.

Cromwell finally found a willing woman in the form of Lady Anne of Cleves. Cleves was a small dukedom in northern Germany, and Anne's brother, the Duke of Cleves, was, like Henry an enemy of the Emperor Charles V. Cromwell was pleased to make an ally who would stand beside England if Charles caused trouble, but Henry's only concern was whether the girl was pretty. The great court painter Holbein was dispatched to Cleves to paint her, so that Henry could see what she looked like before he agreed to the marriage. The portrait must have satisfied Henry because as soon as he saw it the marriage treaty was completed.

The picture shows a demure, dreamy girl, with her hands folded tidily on her tummy. Her eyes have a far-away gaze.

She set off from Dusseldorf in November 1539, accompanied by 263 people and 228 horses. They made a very slow, and probably reluctant, journey to Calais, travelling no more than five miles a day. Anne then remained in Calais for 16 days, waiting for the wind to change, until at last she set sail on a ship decked with banners and streamers and flags.

The plan was that she would meet Henry at Blackheath on 3 January. On the way, Anne spent New Year at the Bishop's Palace in Rochester in Kent. For her entertainment there was a bull-fight in the courtyard, and Anne was watching it from her chamber window when six men burst into her room. They were dressed in identical multicoloured cloaks and their faces were hidden by hoods. One of the men came straight up to Anne and kissed her. He tried to give her a present,

"A token, Madam, from the King."

Anne blushed and stepped backwards. "Thank you," she said. It was one of the few words she knew in English. She then turned back to the window, trying to look fascinated by the bull-fight.

But the intruder would not leave her alone. He tried to stroke her cheek, and run his arms across her back. He kissed her neck. Anne was excruciatingly embarrassed. Who *was* this man? How could she stop him without seeming rude? She had never been touched by a man before. What kind of country was this? And what would the King think if he knew? She stood completely still, and stared out of the window. The man then slapped her on the bottom, and swung out of the chamber, the other five following him.

Anne flopped into a chair. Outside the room was the sound of laughter and commotion. Then trumpets. The doors flew open. The mystery man revealed himself, now dressed in a great coat of purple velvet. He was the King. Anne leapt to her feet, and then fell to her knees in a deep curtsy.

But the King was actually furious that Anne had not responded to him when he was in his disguise. As soon as he had shown his true identity, he left. He didn't give her the New Year's gift of jewelled furs which he had brought. It was a poor start and things were not to improve.

Their wedding was scheduled for the 4th of January. Henry ordered Cromwell to find a way out which would not be a diplomatic disaster. His worry was that if Anne were offended, her brother, the Duke of Cleves, would turn to Henry's enemy Charles V. Henry delayed the wedding, but he quickly saw that there was no escape. They were married on Tuesday the 6th of January. The Queen's gown was made of cloth of gold, embroidered with flowers made of pearls. Her long "yellow" hair was loose beneath a golden coronet decorated with sprigs of rosemary.

It was a brief marriage. All over in six months. Now that he was Supreme Head of the Church of England Henry was of course able to divorce anyone he wanted. This time the process only took three days. Anne did not protest, no doubt relieved to be getting away with her head still attached to her shoulders. She never returned to Cleves, apparently afraid of her brother's anger now that her grand marriage had failed. She spent the rest of her life living quietly in England, and outlived Henry by ten years.

They were divorced on the grounds that their marriage was never consummated – in other words that they never had sex. Their private life was clearly a rum business. Henry had tried night after night to sleep with Anne but claimed that "He found her body in such sort disordered and indisposed to excite and provoke any lust in him."

She, meanwhile, claimed to be unable to understand why she was not pregnant: "Why, when he comes to bed, he kisses me and taketh me by the hand and biddeth me 'Goodnight Sweatheart'; and in the morning he kisses me and biddeth me 'Farewell, Darling'. Is it not enough?"

It was not enough and some thought the fact that Anne did not know that it was not enough might be part of the problem. Henry made it clear to his courtiers that he thought the failure of their new relationship was Anne's fault not his. He felt sure that he would be able "to do the act" with another woman, and just to prove it to himself he started a new romance.

CHAPTER FIFTEEN
Catherine Howard

Henry's new love was Catherine Howard. She was a member of one of the big Howard clan, a cousin of Anne Boleyn, and a niece of the Duke of Norfolk who had found himself forced to condemn Anne to death. There have always been suspicions that the Howard family, having lost influence over Henry when he turned against Anne, deliberately placed another young female member of the family in his way, hoping that through her they could return to power. If that was the plan, it worked, briefly.

Catherine was a lively teenager. At the age of 12, her mother had died and she had been sent to live with her step-grandmother, the very grand, very rich, Dowager Duchess of Norfolk. The old lady ran an enormous household, and took on the upbringing of a large number of distantly related girls who slept, two to a bed, in a huge dormitory called the "Maidens' Chamber". By day they were taught music and reading and writing by teams of young men employed by the Duchess. It was like being brought up in a holiday camp. There were rules: the young men and women were never to be alone together; the men were never to enter the Maidens' Chamber; but the rules were frequently broken. Catherine was given two or three blows by the old lady for being caught alone with the music master Henry Manox.

She was one of the wildest and most daring of the girls, and Manox was desperately in love with her. So was another gentleman of the household: Francis Dereham, and Catherine was very excited by him. She persuaded the Duchess's maid, Mary Lascelles, to steal the key of the Maidens' Chamber so that she could unlock it at night to let Francis Dereham in. Manox was distraught, and told the Duchess of their high jinks: "They commonly banquet and be merry there till two or three of the clock in the morning, drinking wine and eating strawberries, apples and other things to make good cheer." Catherine was called before the duchess for a ticking off: "These late nights will hurt your beauty!" the old lady warned. Catherine politely apologised, but carried on.

When Catherine was 19 she was offered the post of Anne of Cleve's Lady-in-Waiting. She leapt at the chance to go to Court. Dereham begged her not to go, but Catherine was not going to let her lover stand in the way of her career. She glowed with energy and high spirits, and it was not long before she made her next conquest: the King. He was 30 years older than her, grossly obese and in appalling health, but there was no doubt: he was the biggest catch in the country.

Henry was now only able to walk with the aid of a stick. He was tormented by his painful, foul-smelling leg ulcers. He spent much of his time concocting potions to cure his ailments, including an "oyntment… to cool and dry and comfort the member." He was besotted with Catherine and showered her with jewels. At their wedding, which took place on the 28th of July 1540, 16 days after the divorce from Anne, he gave her a golden headdress decorated with seven diamonds, seven rubies and seven pearls; a necklace containing 29 rubies and 29 clusters of pearls, each cluster being composed of four pearls. There was also a gold pendant with a "table diamond", "a very fair ruby" and "a long pearl". In October, to celebrate the first anniversary of meeting her, he gave her more jewels, and then at Christmas a necklace with 33 diamonds, 60 rubies and a border of pearls as well as bejewelled fur scarf.

The King was, at last, in love again. It was, for Catherine, a very dangerous situation. For Henry's passion was murderous when those he loved let him down. Indeed on the very day that Catherine and Henry married, his indispensable assistant, Thomas Cromwell, was beheaded. *His* mistake had been to arrange the unfortunate marriage to Anne of Cleves.

Henry's infatuation with Catherine Howard lasted a year. It was a happy year. Catherine brought Henry together with his children for the first time. When she became Queen only Prince Edward was allowed at court, but she fetched Anne Boleyn's daughter Elizabeth, who was now eight, to join them, and Mary, who was four years older than her new stepmother, was allowed to live at court for the first time since her parents' marriage had broken down.

However, in the autumn of 1541 Archbishop Cramner decided it was his duty to tell the King about the rumours running through court about Catherine. Scared of Henry's reaction to the news, Cranmer left a letter on Henry's seat in chapel. Francis Dereham "hath lied in bed with her in his doublet and hose between the sheets a hundred nights." Henry Manox "knew a privy mark of her body".

At first Henry refused to believe these accusations. He decided to investigate secretly. Dereham and Manox and others in Catherine's circle were interrogated. The investigations took place on Saturday the 5th of November 1541, and they lasted one day. The investigators uncovered the details they needed. One lady's maid said she was sure that Dereham and Catherine had been lovers, for she had "seen them kiss after a wonderful manner, for they would kiss and hang by their bills (lips) together (as if) they were two sparrows". Dereham himself confessed that he had been "six or seven times in naked bed with her".

Henry was struck dumb. Finally, according to the investigators, he broke down in floods of tears, "which" they said "was strange in one of his courage". He never saw Catherine again. He fled to London in the middle of the night, leaving a nervous Catherine in Hampton Court. She knew something was wrong, but she had not yet been told what. On the Monday morning a delegation headed by Cranmer arrived and put the allegations to her. At first she denied everything but, soon realising the strength of the evidence against her, she confessed. She begged for the King's forgiveness for her crime of concealing her "former faults". A Queen was not meant to have ever had any lover other than the King.

Catherine became completely hysterical. She was terrified of being killed. Cranmer reported back to Henry that she was in such a state "that it would have pitied any man's heart to have looked upon her". Henry was inclined to be merciful so long as he could be sure that she had been true to him once they were married. The investigations continued, but Catherine was now panicking. Since coming to court she had fallen in love with another man. A distant cousin called Thomas Culpepper. A young and beautiful man. Unaware of the circling danger Culpepper was away from court, "merry ahawking". Praying that their secret would not come out, Catherine could not hide her fear. Three or four times a day she asked for news of him. Eventually it came. Culpepper had been arrested. On the rack Dereham had confessed to sleeping with Catherine before her marriage. But he had not slept with her since then, he insisted, for she had left him for Culpepper.

Immediately Catherine was questioned again and Culpepper was arrested. Both, it seems, told the truth, for their accounts agree. There had been gifts, rings and bracelets, and secret meetings in lavatories and back stairs. They had told each other they loved each other. He had kissed her hand, "saying he would presume no further." It was far enough. Dereham and Culpepper were tried for treason on 1 December, and found guilty. Dereham, for the crime of having slept naked with Catherine when they were both unmarried and before

she knew she would ever be Queen, was hanged, cut down still alive, castrated, disembowelled, beheaded and quartered. Culpepper, coming from a grander family, was simply beheaded.

Catherine was kept under house arrest. Interviewed early in the new year she "openly confessed" her "great crime", and asked just two things: that her family would not be condemned with her, and that the King give some of her fine clothes to her attendants after her death. She was taken, like Anne Boleyn, by river to the Tower. She fought and struggled hopelessly, and once in the Tower it was reported "she weeps and cries and torments herself miserably, without ceasing". She was to have her head chopped off by an axe, and to prepare herself she asked for the execution block to be brought to her room so that she could try it out.

When the time of her execution came, Catherine made a full apology to God. She said she had broken every one of his commandments. She called on the people to obey the King in all things. She knelt down and put her head on the block. She was 21 years old.

As soon as Catherine's head was off, it was the turn of her companion, Lady Rochford, the woman who had helped organise the secret meetings with Culpepper. She appeared deranged until the final moment when she too quietly put her head on the block. She was at last joining her husband Lord Rochford, the brother of Anne Boleyn, who had been executed in the same place, six years earlier.

CHAPTER SIXTEEN
Return to War

Betrayed in love, Henry turned to war. Wales had already been brought under Henry's control, and more recently Henry had declared himself King of Ireland. Scotland, however, remained fiercely independent and there were skirmishes on the border, as bands of Scots attacked English villages. In Europe, meanwhile, Charles V was at war with the French again. Henry saw the opportunity to patch up his relationship with Charles by diving into the action against France.

Although he was in the middle of trying to negotiate a marriage between his daughter Mary and a French prince, Henry decided to launch an attack on France with Charles V. At the same time he sent an army to invade Scotland. The shock killed the king of Scotland, James V. Although he wasn't injured in battle, he collapsed and died three weeks later, leaving his daughter Mary to become Queen of the Scots. She was one week old.

Henry thought that with a tiny baby as Queen, Scotland would now be very easy to take over. His first plan was to arrange a marriage between the baby girl and his six-year-old son, Edward. That way Edward would end up as King of Scotland. Not surprisingly, the Scots didn't fall for that scheme, so Henry decided to launch another furious attack. He ordered that Edinburgh be destroyed and all the men, women, and children killed. There were ten days of bitter violence, but Henry was never able to gain control of Scotland.

Nor was he successful in France. He planned to capture Paris, but only succeeded in taking control of the much smaller city of Boulogne. The cost of this war almost bankrupted him, and in the end he sold the town back to the French for two million crowns. Henry was now 57. His fighting days were over. He never put on his massive armour again.

CHAPTER SEVENTEEN
Catherine Parr

After the execution of Catherine Howard it took Henry just over a year to find a new wife. This time he chose a very different kind of woman. Catherine Parr was 31, much older than Catherine Howard, though still 21 years younger than Henry. She had been twice widowed, but had no children. She came from a family of courtiers, and at the time Henry first took a fancy to her, she was in love with Thomas Seymour, one of Jane Seymour's brothers. However, when the King chose her to be his wife she had to give up her love and do as commanded. Seymour waited for her, and in fact when Henry died, four years later, she promptly married him, and immediately became pregnant for the first time in her life. Her happiness was brief. Like Jane Seymour, Catherine developed a fever after giving birth. She died four days later at the age of 36.

Like Henry's first two wives Catherine was a very intelligent woman – too intelligent for Henry's liking. She was well educated and had strong views on religion, and unlike Henry she took the modern Protestant line. She even wrote a prayer book, which was an extraordinary thing to do at a time when no women wrote books and all women were supposed to look to their husbands for wisdom. And she had the scariest husband of them all.

One evening in March 1546 she went to see Henry in his apartments. The King was by now too lame to visit the Queen's chambers, which was the normal custom. Henry was sitting grumpily with his ulcerated leg resting on a foot stool. Catherine thought it would comfort him to talk about God, but Henry could barely hide his irritation. He politely bid her farewell, and as soon as she had gone he exploded with sarcasm:"A good hearing it is when women become such clerks, and a thing much to my comfort, to come in mine old days to be taught by my wife! I shall be rid of her!"

Henry's dutiful advisors immediately made plans for

her arrest. Luckily someone warned Catherine and she went straight back to Henry's chambers.

Henry decided to test her. "Tell me, sweetheart, what think you of how a man should save his soul?"

"My Lord, I pray you not to ask my opinion, for I am only a silly poor woman, so much inferior in all respects of nature unto you, and must I, will I, refer my judgement in this, and all other cases to Your Majesty's wisdom, as my only anchor, Supreme Head and Governor here in earth, next under God." She bowed her head deeply.

"Not so by St. Mary. You are become a doctor, Kate, to instruct us, and not to be instructed or directed by us," Henry taunted.

"No, my Lord. I have only disputed with your Majesty, so that you might correct my faults and instruct me with your marvellous learned arguments, and, my Lord, I hoped that such conversation would take your mind from your body's pain."

"And is it even so, sweetheart?" cried Henry.

Her performance had saved her life. Henry forgave her. Catherine had hidden her feelings for Thomas Seymour; now she hid her religious beliefs. She played the submissive wife until Henry died – which was just a few months later.

Henry's funeral was magnificent. The coffin, draped in blue velvet and cloth of gold, was so huge that the roads between Whitehall and Windsor were widened to let it pass. On top of the coffin was a life-size waxwork model of the King, dressed in crimson velvet, wearing a crown and glittering jewellery.

Henry had left instructions for his burial. He wanted to be buried in the Lady Chapel at Windsor Castle, beside Jane Seymour, in an extravagant tomb of black marble with golden angels that Thomas Wolsey had started to build for himself. Henry had had the disgraced Wolsey buried in Leicester, and had planned to rob his servant of his grave as well as his palaces. However, Wolsey's grand tomb had never been finished, so instead Jane Seymour's grave was opened up and Henry's enormous coffin placed in it beside her.

For many years there were strange rumours about the King's body. Some said that his corpse was so full of poison that it exploded and that, shortly before his burial, it burst out of his coffin, spraying the church with fat and pus and blood. Others said that during the reign of his daughter Mary his body was stolen and burnt, on her command, as a punishment for leaving the Catholic Church.

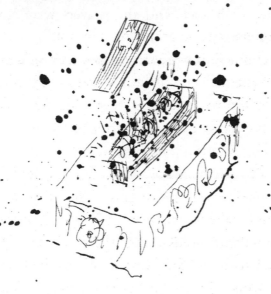

What is certain is that Henry's plans for the care of his body and soul after his death were never carried out. After the burial, work was restarted on the grand tomb. However, the expensive work was abandoned during the reign of Henry's son Edward VI and his coffin was never transferred. Hoping to make sure that he got a place in heaven, Henry had left money to pay for daily prayers to be said for his soul "while the world should endure". This was an old Catholic practice, and of course it was Henry who had taken England out of the

Catholic Church. The Protestants who now controlled the Church of England did not agree that money could buy a place in heaven and the prayers were stopped after only a year.

If he did not get to heaven, Henry had only himself to blame.

TIMELINE

1491, *28th June*: Henry VIII is born.

1502: Brother Arthur dies, leaving Henry as heir

1509: Henry VII dies, leaving Henry VIII as king. Henry marries Katharine of Aragon.

1512: Attacks on France begin.

1516: Katharine gives birth to Mary

1520: Henry meets with Charles V of Spain, and then Francois I of France.

1527: Anne Boleyn becomes unofficial First Lady at public appearances.

1530: Wolsey supposedly poisoned.

1532: Henry illegally marries Anne in secret.

1533: Anne becomes pregnant and gives birth to Elizabeth.

1534: Henry creates the Church of England in order to divorce Katharine.

1535: closing of monasteries, and killing of the non-converted begins.

1536, *January*: Katharine supposedly poisoned. Henry falls for Jane Seymour. Executes Anne under suspicion of adultery, making Elizabeth illegitimate.

    25th May: Henry and Jane marry.

1537: Henry executes rebels including Robert Aske.

1540   *6 January*: Henry marries Anne of Cleves.

    12th July: they divorce.

    28th July: Henry marries Catherine Howard.

1542: Catherine executed for adultery.

1543: Henry marries Catherine Parr.

1547: Henry dies and is buried beside Jane Seymour. Henry's son, Edward VI, is proclaimed king.

QUIZ

After you've finished the book, test yourself and see how well you remember what you've read.

1. When Henry was a young boy, his mother would:
   Tell him stories of kings and knights
   Beat him if he didn't say his prayers
   Force him to eat spinach three times a day

2. In 1497 Henry and his siblings were sent to the Tower of London because:
   They refused to do their Latin homework
   London was under attack from an army of Cornishmen and it was a safe place
   Their parents thought they would be amused by the prisoners in the dungeons

3. Henry was good at lots of sports and particularly enjoyed:
   The new and popular game of netball
   Playing football in his specially made boots
   The ancient pastime of clay-pigeon shooting

4. A typical day for the young king Henry started with:

A light breakfast and prayer

A feast of meat, fish and wine

A naked swim in the River Thames

5. When Henry went off to fight a war in France, Katharine of Aragon:

Held all-night parties in the palace with her Spanish friends

Fought and defeated 10,000 Scottish troops

Took the opportunity to pay a visit to her aged parents

6. The lavish expense laid on for Henry VIII and Charles V's meeting at the Field of the Cloth of Gold in1520 was designed to:

Show the Americans that Europe was a significant military power

Cement the friendship between France and England

Provide a boost to the economy of northern France

7. What did Henry do when Anne Boleyn rejected his advances?

He wrote her lots of passionate love letters

He ordered that she be locked up in prison

He went to the royal agony aunt for advice

8. The Lord Chancellor, Thomas Wolsey, called Anne Boleyn:

A right cow

A sight for sore eyes

A night crow

9. When Katharine of Aragon died, Henry:

Realised he'd made a terrible mistake and that he'd always loved her

Put on his fine clothes and went off to church with a fanfare of trumpets

Commissioned a statue to ensure her memory would live forever

10. As Supreme Head of the Church of England, Henry wished to:

Erase any mention of the Pope from all the prayer books in the country

Ensure that a spirit of tolerance and forgiveness spread throughout the land

Enable women to become priests and celebrate communion

11. When he wanted to divorce her, Henry claimed that Anne Boleyn had had an affair with:

The abbot of Langdon Abbey in Kent

The person who delivered milk to the royal palace

The man who wiped the king's bottom

12. Henry delayed Anne's execution for two days so that:

He could arrange for a quickie divorce

She could attend her daughter Elizabeth's birthday party

Her elderly parents could be present for the occasion

13. How was news of Jane Seymour's pregnancy celebrated in 1537?

A national competition to guess the name of the baby was announced

Bonfires were lit throughout the land

Every boy under the age of 11 was given a bar of chocolate

14. In order to put down rebellion in the north of England:

Henry invited the leader to stay at his house for Christmas

Handed the territory over to the King of Scotland

Offered his daughter Elizabeth's hand in marriage to anyone who could defeat the rebels

15. Henry found out what Anne of Cleves looked like before he agreed to marry her by:

Getting her to fill in a questionnaire about her appearance

Asking his little sister to make friends with her and report back

Sending the court painter Holbein to paint her portrait

16. Catherine Howard's grandmother, the Dowager Duchess of Norfolk, encouraged the young women in her household to:

Learn how to read and write

Stay up late playing cards

Volunteer to help children at the local school

17. How long after his divorce from Anne was Henry's marriage to Catherine?

16 days

16 weeks

16 months

18. After Henry's fifth wife Catherine Howard confessed to adultery she asked him to:

Let her be killed by a Frenchman so the death would be quick

Give away her fine clothes to her attendants
Scatter her ashes in the Thames

19. For Henry's funeral the roads between Windsor and
Whitechapel were widened so that:
    Henry's enormous coffin could pass through
    More people to come and watch
    A jousting match could take place after the event

20. Henry's last wife, Catherine Parr, wrote:
    A prayer book
    A history of the Tudor dynasty
    A candid account of her life as a queen

BIBLIOGRAPHY

John Bowle, *Henry VIII* (Allen and Unwin, 1964).
Christopher Falkus, *The Private Lives of the Tudor Monarchs* (London Folio Society, 1974)
Peter Gwyn, *The King's Cardinal* (Barry and Jenkins, 1990)
Adam Hart-Davis, *What the Tudors and Stuarts did for us (Boxtree 2002)*
Jasper Ridley, *Henry VIII* (Constable, 1985)
J.J. Scarisbrick, *Henry VIII* (Eyre, Metheun 1968)
David Starkey, *Six Wives* (Vintage 2004)
David Starkey, *The Reign of Henry VIII* (Collins and Brown, 1991)
Alison Weir, *Henry VIII* (Cape, 2001)

www.learningcurve.gov.uk
www.historylearningsite.co.uk

Dear Reader,

No matter how old you are, good books always leave you wanting to know more. If you have any questions you would like to ask the author, **Emma Craigie,** about **Henry VIII** please write to us at: SHORT BOOKS, 15 Highbury Terrace, London N5 1UP.

If you enjoyed this title, then you would probably enjoy others in the series. Why not click on our website for more information and see what the teachers are being told?
www.shortbooks.co.uk

All the books in the WHO WAS... series are available from TBS, Distribution Centre, Colchester Road, Frating Green, Colchester, Essex CO7 7DW
(Tel: 01206 255800), at £4.99 + P&P.

AUTHOR BIOGRAPHY

Emma Craigie is a writer and teacher who lives in Somerset
with her husband and four children

ACKNOWLEDGEMENTS

I would like to thank Jess Bell, David Craigie, Maud Craigie
and Chris Culpin for their support and advice.